Original title:
Shoreline Serenity

Copyright © 2025 Creative Arts Management OÜ
All rights reserved.

Author: Henry Beaumont
ISBN HARDBACK: 978-1-80581-598-3
ISBN PAPERBACK: 978-1-80581-125-1
ISBN EBOOK: 978-1-80581-598-3

## **Nature's Quiet Embrace**

Seagulls squawking, quite the show,
Dropping snacks, now that's a blow!
Crabs in tuxedos dance about,
As waves of laughter roll and shout.

Sandy toes and sun-kissed noses,
Tickling waves, who needs the roses?
Unruly kids, their joy runs wild,
Even grumpy dads can't help but smile.

## Surrender to the Lull of the Ocean

Waves yawn softly, just a tease,
As fishy friends do belly sneeze.
Flip-flops fly in sandy storms,
Frolicking like a herd of norms.

Buckets tip with laughter bright,
Ice cream melts, oh what a sight!
Seashells giggle, hiding near,
With every splash, joy draws us near.

## Coastal Serenity Captured in Time

Dolphins leap and do a spin,
While tourists chase their tail fins in.
Sunsets spill like grape juice spilled,
On sandy canvas, laughter thrilled.

Beach balls bounce with silly grace,
An octopus joins the race!
Laughter bubbles in salty air,
Squished sandwiches everywhere!

## The Art of Stillness at the Water's Edge

Sitting still with ice cream heaps,
While whales swim by in funny leaps.
Turtles ponder, looking wise,
While wind whispers its goofy sighs.

Fish wear hats, or so I think,
As waves bring joy with every wink.
A crab declares it's time to dance,
Who knew a tide could lead a prance!

## **Beneath the Canopy of Clouds**

Beneath the clouds so fluffy and white,
Seagulls are squawking, what a delight!
A beach ball's bouncing, oh what a chase,
As kids go flying all over the place.

Flip-flops skip like frogs in a race,
While sandcastles wobble at a quick pace.
A beachside picnic, how grand, oh my!
Someone just spilled the lemonade – oh, why!

## **Trinkets of Tranquility**

Shells and stones, treasures galore,
A hermit crab wins the race to the shore.
We gather our finds, all sparkly and bright,
Counting our trinkets, what a silly sight!

But watch out for waves, they sneak up so sly,
A sudden splash makes everyone cry.
Laughter erupts, and in moments like these,
We all look like soggy sandwiches, oh please!

## **Moonlit Reflections on the Water**

Under the moon, the water does gleam,
Where fish in tuxedos may be a dream.
Two turtles play cards, with shells as their chairs,
As crabs offer snacks from the seas' hidden lairs.

A dolphin shows up, thinking he's slick,
Practicing flips—oh, that synchronized trick!
But falls with a splash, much to our delight,
The sea's got more hiccups than we planned for tonight!

### A Melody of Seashell Scents

The scents of the sea drift into the air,
Sandwiches left out, not a single care.
Seashells whistling, a peculiar tune,
Making us giggle beneath the bright moon.

A crab in a bowtie joins in the song,
While mermaids complain it's taking too long.
We dance around wildly, to waves' steady beat,
Even the seaweed seems to tap its own feet!

## Basket of Clouds Adrift on Blue

A basket of clouds in the sky,
Wobbly like jelly, oh my!
They float by like a bunch of ducks,
While sunbeams play silly tricks.

A seagull steals a donut from a kid,
The child shrieks, oh what a bid!
The gull laughs, a beak filled with cream,
While the kid dreams of ice cream.

## A Mosaic of Ocean's Colors

Waves splashing like paint in a mess,
A crab in a tux, oh what finesse!
He dances with shells, a rhythmic spree,
While a fish chuckles, 'Come join me!'

Seaweed sways like a jazzy band,
With conch shells gossiping, oh isn't it grand?
A dolphin dives in, flips with flair,
While a starfish just lounges, no care.

## Calmness Holding Hands with Time

The clock ticks softly, a gentle friend,
Ocean whispers secrets, around the bend.
A turtle, very slow, takes its time,
Saying, 'Hurry? Now that's a crime!'

With a wink, the tide sets the pace,
While crabs have a race, it's a silly chase.
Laughing at moments that drift like foam,
In this quiet place, we all feel at home.

## Serenity Found in the Salty Air

The waves are giggling, can you hear?
Shells are laughing, spreading cheer.
Seagulls dance with goofy grace,
Crabs are prancing all over the place.

Sandcastles melt like dreams in sun,
A flip-flop's gone, what a funny run!
The beach ball bounces, oh what a sight,
Kites drop down like they're taking flight.

## Embracing the Echoes of the Ocean

The ocean murmurs secrets low,
While dolphins tease the tide to and fro.
A jellyfish wobbles with great delight,
And starfish giggle under moonlight.

Seagulls shout their jokes aloud,
While beachgoers laugh, feeling proud.
An octopus tickles a curious kid,
Who squeals with joy, his fears all hid.

## Sunsets Brushed by Gentle Waves

The sun dips down with genteel flair,
Painting the sky without a care.
Paddleboards wobble, folks take a dive,
Splashing and giggling, feeling alive.

Mermaids whisper silly rhymes,
Counting all the seagull's crimes.
A splash of water, a snort of glee,
As seaweed wraps 'round a hapless knee.

## **The Peace of Tides Turned**

Tides keep turning in a playful dance,
While flip-flops chase, oh what a chance!
A surfboard wobbles, then goes kaboom,
Filling the air with an air of gloom.

Sun-kissed faces with sandy grins,
Waving at fish as the laughter begins.
A seagull steals a sandwich with flair,
While we all chuckle at our own despair.

## **Beneath the Azure Waves**

Beneath the waves, a crab does dance,
In a tuxedo shell, he takes a chance.
Fish in bow ties swim by with glee,
They laugh at the waves, oh so carefree.

Starfish throw parties, they rarely sleep,
Jellyfish jive while the sea lions peep.
Mermaids roll their eyes at the silly show,
They try to join in, but just float and glow.

## Tranquil Reflections at Dusk

As dusk descends, the gulls take flight,
Fish are wearing their best, what a sight!
With splashy splashes, they vie for the prize,
A sandcastle winner in silly disguise.

The moon chuckles down on the sandy floor,
While crabs in a conga line scuttle and soar.
"Who knew the sea could throw such a bash?"
They dance in the surf with a glimmering splash.

## Gentle Lullabies of the Sea

The sea hums softly, a tune so sweet,
While starfish doze off, curled up in their seat.
A whale taps the beat with its huge tail,
And dolphins join in with a giggly wail.

With barnacles snoring, a sleepy affair,
The hermit crabs gossip, without a care.
"What's for breakfast? A shell or a snack?"
The ocean echoes with laughter, 'Let's not slack!'

## The Embrace of Ocean's Breath

The ocean's breath tickles the coast,
As seaweed wiggles, it makes its boast.
"Look at me!" shouts a clam with pride,
"I'm the best at hiding, come take a ride!"

Octopuses juggle, it's quite a sight,
They drop all their balls in a fit of delight.
Seagulls squawk jokes that are 'fowl', it's true,
The beachgoers giggle, as they all pursue.

## Crashing Whispers

Waves giggle as they kiss the sand,
Seagulls squawk, they're part of the band.
A crab dances sideways, oh what a sight,
Turtles in swimsuits, trying to look right.

Shells collect stories, so many they tell,
A hermit now wears a fancy hotel.
Fish laugh as they wiggle, swim 'round in delight,
While the sun gives a wink, it's a warm, silly sight.

## **Silent Shores**

Clouds wear mustaches, drifting on high,
And the sun's in flip-flops, oh my, oh my!
The tide whispers jokes while it's rolling in,
Sandcastles giggle, let the fun begin!

A flip-flop party beneath palm tree fronds,
Where the beachcombers dance with colorful wands.
Even the starfish have a dance to share,
Life at the edge is light as the air!

## A Haven of Horizon's Embrace

Palm trees do the cha-cha, so jazzy and fun,
While the ocean plays tag with the rays of sun.
Seagull sportscasters shout from above,
Each wave a new scoop, oh what a love!

The beach towels laugh, embracing each friend,
With ice cream smiles that never quite end.
Shells offer a tea party for creatures so shy,
Under the warm watch of the summer sky.

## Drifted Wishes on the Beach

Footprints giggle as the tide steals away,
Each grain of sand has a secret to say.
Starfish wish on wishing wells made of foam,
Crabs wave good luck as they drift far from home.

The dunes wear hats made of wildflowers bright,
As the sun plays peek-a-boo, what a delight!
Shells whisper tales of the creatures they know,
While the waves tickle toes, putting on a show.

## **Peace at Waters' Edge**

The breeze is a joker, playful and spry,
Clouds play hide and seek in the endless sky.
Seashells throw parties, they know how to cheer,
Laughing with dolphins, bringing joy near.

In this wacky corner where sea meets the land,
Fish toss confetti, the fun is so grand.
Time takes a break, just to join in the fun,
At this silly place where the laughter's begun.

### Little Secrets Beneath the Water's Veil

Bubbles giggle as they rise,
Fish wear glasses, oh so wise!
Crabs are dancing, what a sight,
Seahorses twirl in sheer delight.

Starfish gossip, arms entwined,
Clams make cookies, one of a kind.
Jellyfish float like happy kites,
Aquatic jokes and silly bites.

## Ripples of Calm Where Fishes Play

Goldfish joke in tiny schools,
Wearing hats, they break the rules.
Turtles skate on ocean's floor,
Waves applauding, begging for more.

Bubbles pop like party cheers,
As dolphins share their goofball fears.
Eels tell tales of slimy grace,
Seagulls chuckle, they love the race.

## Resonance of Peace in Shells' Embrace

Shells sing softly, pure and clear,
They whisper secrets, lend an ear.
Clams play cards with crabs at night,
Their laughter echoes, pure delight.

Oysters holding talent shows,
They dazzle, then strike funny poses.
A lobster's joke brings waves of glee,
The ocean's heart is wild and free.

**Beneath the Canopy of Stars**

Starfish dream of candy bars,
While shrimp debate on who they are.
The moonlight winks, a playful light,
Waves laugh hard, it feels so right.

Octopi wear socks with flair,
Mermaids dance without a care.
The night is filled with silly sound,
Where humor mixed with joy is found.

## Whispers of the Tides

The seagulls squawk, they crack jokes,
As waves tickle feet like playful folks.
Sandcastles wobble, they sway and sway,
Who knew that tides could dance and play?

Crabs in tuxedos, they strut with pride,
Hitching a ride on the fish tide slide.
Starfish giggle, they wiggle around,
In this salty circus, joy knows no bound.

Sunscreen's on but so is the sand,
My beach hat flew; now it's lost in the land.
Flip-flops flying, what a wild spree,
In this sandy world, we all feel free.

As twilight falls, the laughter goes wide,
The ocean's a friend, never a guide.
From splashes of joy, to slips on the wet,
This shore's a place I'll never forget.

## Calm Beneath the Horizon

Beneath the calm where the seagulls lay,
Turtles in shades enjoy their day.
A fish on a surfboard, what a sight,
Waving at dolphins in pure delight.

Buckets and shovels build castles grand,
With moats for the crabs, who make a stand.
Kids splash and giggle, their laughter flows,
While sunburned dads trade bad dad jokes.

The tide rolls in, it's a slippery race,
As flip-flops fly, oh what a chase!
Meanwhile, a sandpiper sings offbeat,
In this sandy jam, we tap our feet.

When the sun dips low, all voices blend,
As hermit crabs crawl, seeking friends.
With waves laughing softly, we take a bow,
For in this fun place, we live in the now.

## Gentle Embrace of Waves

Waves giggle gently, a tickle parade,
They tease little kids, in water they wade.
Buckets and spades, a child's delight,
As sunburnt toes dance in the light.

A seal wears glasses, sunbathing slow,
While jellyfish float, putting on a show.
Mermaids are laughing, or so they claim,
In this cozy cove, it's all just a game.

Kites soar above, as seagulls swoon,
While a clown fish dreams of being a boon.
Sandy sunbathers, all piled high,
Find peace in the chaos of laughter and sighs.

With each crashing wave, comes a declaration,
"Frolicking here is our favorite vacation!"
As stars glimmer down and the ocean hums,
In this playful world, we all feel young.

## Reflections on the Sand

Footprints drawing paths, in a zig-zag line,
As children dig deep, searching for treasure divine.
The tide whispers secrets, a funny old tale,
Of a pirate's lost sock washed up on the trail.

A pelican stately with fishy delight,
Shares tales of escape from the gull's silly flight.
Shells gleam with laughter in hues bold and bright,
As beach balls bounce, igniting the night.

With sunburned noses and goofy grins wide,
We set our umbrellas, it's a colorful ride.
While chuckling waves roll, bringing stories anew,
In this wacky expanse, there's room for the crew.

As night cloaks the day, and the stars start to sing,
We dance with the shadows, let laughter take wing.
In reflections of joy, we'll always understand,
Life's better together, on this fun, sandy land.

**Sunsets Sown in Soft Sand**

Golden rays gleam, what a sight,
Seagulls dance, they're taking flight.
Buckets spill sand, kids in a race,
Chasing waves with messy grace.

Flip-flops flying, laughter rings,
Splashing water, oh the fun it brings!
Sandcastles lean, a little too proud,
While crabs scuttle, escaping the crowd.

Tropical drinks in their coconuts,
Stumbling beach chairs, oh what a fuss!
Sunsets painted, colors collide,
A jellyfish floats, on a lazy tide.

## The Quiet Pulse of the Bay

Dinghies bobbing, tethered tight,
A squirrel sneaks by with a curious bite.
Sun-glazed waters, a splash and a flop,
Fish flipping around like they're part of a prop.

Pelicans diving, taking a dip,
One landed hard, oh what a trip!
Sunscreen slip-ups, that's quite a sight,
While beach umbrellas take flight with delight.

Sandwiches squished in the picnic pack,
Ants find them first, we've lost our snack!
A crab doing yoga, in search of a tan,
Who knew that a beach could be so unplanned?

## **Whispers of the Tidal Breeze**

Waves whisper secrets, a gentle tease,
While beach balls bounce with the utmost ease.
A lighthouse winks, it's quite a charmer,
Sending boats home, like a friendly farmer.

Kites are flying, crazy and wild,
A runaway hat claims a beachside child.
Watermelon slices, sweet and ripe,
Sticky fingers, such a summer type.

Sandy toes giggle with each stride,
A rogue wave laughs, it's a joyride!
Flip-flops fall, what a hilarious scene,
Chasing the tide like a lively routine.

## Echoes of the Calm Coast

Seashells gossip, what tales they tell,
As flip-flops clack, ringing like a bell.
A sunburned dad, with a grilling plan,
Grabbing a hot dog, like a true beachman.

Surfers wobble, poised like a crane,
Fall in the waves, then get up again.
Picnic blankets, a little too neat,
Until a seagull swoops down for a treat.

Evening bonfires, laughter ignites,
Someone's pants catch the flames, what a sight!
Under starry skies, the moon takes its cue,
With whispers of memories meant just for you.

## Beneath the Surf's Soft Caress

Waves giggle as they crash and play,
Tickling toes that dance in sway.
Seagulls squawk, they steal your fries,
A splash of salt, a sea breeze surprise.

Drifting boats with snacks on board,
Chuckle at the fisherman's horde.
A dolphin pops up, makes a face,
As if to say, 'I win this race!'

Children build castles, dreams so grand,
Only to have the tide make a stand.
They chase the waves, laughter in the air,
As the ocean swallows their sandy lair.

With sun hats flying, delight in the sun,
The beach is a circus, oh what fun!
Mermaids giggle in the foam, so bright,
In this paradise, everything feels right.

## **A Horizon Wrapped in Peace**

Clouds like cotton candy drift away,
While surfers shout, 'I caught a ray!'
Beach balls bounce with a silly clang,
As kids giggle from the flops and tang.

Kites dance wildly, colors collide,
A picnic spread, where joy can't hide.
Sandwiches in hand, what a feast,
The ants throw a party, to say the least!

A crabs' dance-off, oh who's the champ?
They wave their claws, so proud and damp.
Flip-flops fly as the patrons flee,
Chased by water, oh what a spree!

As the sun sinks low and paints the sky,
Beachgoers laugh, let worries fly.
Each sunset a canvas, vivid and bold,
Turning day into stories untold.

## Canvas of Stars Above the Water

Stars twinkle like they lost a bet,
The crab's got jokes, don't you forget!
Laughter echoes along the shore,
As the moon peeks out, wanting more.

Sandcastles glow in the night's embrace,
With a glowstick tower that's out of place.
The tide rolls in with a wave of cheer,
While fish swap tales in whispers near.

Flip-flops become a bouncing game,
Who can hop and not feel shame?
The ocean sighs with a giggle or two,
"Join in the fun!" it calls to you.

With the stars above, we dance and sway,
Under this blanket of milky display.
In the moon's spotlight, we find our way,
With crabs and laughter, we drift till day.

## Glistening Shells and Hushed Secrets

Shells whisper tales of the deep blue yonder,
Of fish with hats and a whale's sweet wander.
A crusty conch claims it's the beach's king,
But a dancing starfish just wants to swing!

Footprints in sand tell stories unknown,
As beachcombers roam, their faces have grown.
"Treasure!" they shout, a bottle, a cap,
But the real prize? A hammock nap!

Waves play tic-tac-toe on the shore,
"X" marks the spot for snacks galore!
Sand to the left, snacks to the right,
As pelicans swoop for a late-night bite.

The moon's a spotlight on this late-night spree,
With giggles bouncing as wild as can be.
And as the tide pulls away with a sigh,
We're left with those tales beneath the sky.

## Calm Reflections in the Estuary

Seagulls squawk as they dive for fries,
An unexpected feast under bright blue skies.
Fish stare up thinking, 'What a day!'
While crabs scuttle around, dreaming of ballet.

The water shimmies in a silly dance,
A jellyfish floats like it's found romance.
But don't get too close to that squishy sight,
It's all fun and games 'til you get a fright!

Laughter echoes as waves crash ashore,
Sandcastles tumble like a child's encore.
With buckets and spades, we dig our dreams,
In this quirky realm where silliness beams.

So let the tide carry our giggles with grace,
As we splash and play in this happy place.
Each ripple and wave, a chuckle or cheer,
In the estuary's arms, there's nothing to fear.

## A Melody of Sand and Sea


The ocean hums a tune with a twist,
A crab starts dancing, you get the gist.
The waves spell out jokes in foamy white,
While seashells giggle, oh what a sight!

Flip-flops flop as we stroll along,
A sunburned nose sings the wrong song.
A starfish winks from its sandy bed,
'Who needs legs when I have these arms instead?'

The surf's a comedian, rolling in glee,
Tickling our toes with a playful spree.
A dolphin leaps high with flair and might,
While I just trip and wipe out in fright.

Yet through all the chaos, the sun shines bright,
We laugh at our blunders under its light.
For in this dance of the sea and the sand,
Every chuckle's a memory perfectly planned.

## Twilight Conversations with the Tide

As the sun slips down with a cheeky grin,
The waves whisper secrets that tease us to spin.
Starfish share tales of their glamorous days,
While crabs create dramas, in comical ways.

The moon peeks in, a curious friend,
'What's happening here? Will the laughter end?'
But the water just giggles, rolling with cheer,
A playful conversation we all hold dear.

Footprints in sand, like lines in a play,
Tell of our antics throughout the day.
With each little splash, there's a punchline anew,
The tide's our audience, and we're the crew.

As twilight fades, we still laugh and joke,
With the rhythm of night, our hearts provoke.
In the quiet we find, an echo of glee,
For every soft wave is a part of this spree.

## The Poetry of Still Waters

In the silence of dusk, where the waters reflect,
A rubber duck swims with perfect respect.
It quacks out a verse, a whimsical line,
While frogs join in chorus, feeling divine.

A dragonfly buzzes, a poet with style,
Dancing on water like it's been a while.
Each ripple expands with laughter and fun,
As crickets serenade beneath the setting sun.

Mirth in the stillness, a playful delight,
With silly old turtles who wonder and bite.
Their shells are their homes; they never quite roam,
But write epic ballads that weave through the foam.

So we gather around this tranquil gold,
And listen for stories the water has told.
In the peace of the moment, our hearts feel the beat,
For laughter and joy are the best forms of heat.

## The Color of Tranquility in Waves

The waves dance like they've lost their shoes,
With seagulls laughing, it's hard to snooze.
Fish flip-flop like they're at a rave,
Ocean breeze whispers, "You'll be my wave!"

Who knew that sand could tickle so right?
Crabs scurry sideways in a comical sight.
Sunbathers blush with radiant glee,
While sandcastles are toppled by kids' wild spree.

Beach balls bouncing, mischief ignites,
Coolers overflowing with delicious bites.
As tides ebb and flow, they tell their joke,
Life's a beach, so let's all provoke!

Glorious sunsets paint the sky with cheer,
Sun sunscreen smudges, we shed a tear.
In the distance, laughter sails away,
Waves nodding, saying, "Stay for the play!"

## Serenity in the Driftwood's Embrace


Driftwood lounging like it's on a chair,
Whispers to the seashells without a care.
"Hey there, buddy! Join me for some sun,"
While crabs plot schemes for a bit of fun.

Pelicans fishing like they're on a spree,
One takes a dive, yelling, "Look at me!"
The tide rolls in, a giggling tease,
As sand wraps 'round toes like a cozy squeeze.

Turtles know how to take their slow stroll,
While dandelion fluff plays hide and roll.
It's a comedy show where vines entwine,
Nature's laughter makes every moment fine.

Every wave brings a new punchline, too,
As umbrellas dance and the beach balls rue.
With every sunset, the colors outplay,
In driftwood's arms, we'll laugh all day!

## The Ocean's Gentle Heartbeat

The ocean pulses like a giant heart,
Beating rhythms as we play our part.
Jellyfish float like clowns in the stream,
As the breeze joins in for a goofy dream.

Waves roll in, a wild tickling spree,
Surfboards tumble, yelling, "Look at me!"
Seashells gossip, sharing their news,
In every splashing wave, laughter ensues.

Sun hats fly off in the warm, salty air,
As seagulls squawk, "Hey, how's your hair?"
Kids catch the surf with squeals of delight,
While sandbars form like a playful fight.

With every crash, the ocean's a bard,
Reciting tales, often quite hard.
Yet together we laugh, our spirits ignite,
In this watery realm, everything feels right.

## Clouds Floating Over Silent Waters

Clouds drift by like marshmallows in flight,
Whispering jokes to the waves in the light.
Silence is funny when funny is found,
In puddles of sunshine where giggles abound.

The waters chuckle, reflecting the show,
As boats bob on down, dancing to and fro.
Fish playing peek-a-boo with a shy grin,
As nature's chorus begins to spin.

With a splash and a dash, the ducks parade,
Waddling proudly, their nonchalance displayed.
The wind plays tricks, tickling the trees,
While everyone laughs, feeling so free.

As day turns to night, the colors depart,
But laughter lingers like a warm, cozy heart.
With soft glowing lights beneath the dark skies,
We'll cherish these moments and share the best highs!

## **Flickering Lights on Calm Waters**

Bobbing boats in goofy dance,
A lighthouse blinks like it has ants.
Seagulls squawk a silly song,
As I trip on sand, can't stay strong.

Twilight paints the sky in pink,
While fish splash water; what's their stink?
I laugh at crabs with sideways stride,
They seem so lost, with nowhere to hide.

Glow of stars lights up my snack,
A sandwich flies – who brought that back?
Jellyfish doing jelly rolls,
While beach balls soar like wayward souls.

So here I sit, in sandy bliss,
With every wave comes sloshing kiss.
Laughter echoes through the night,
As tides keep teasing, out of sight.

## Starlit Paths Along the Beach

Footprints left on sugar sand,
I trip and fall; Oh, wasn't planned!
Stars above my head do wink,
As I ponder, what's for drink?

Bikinis and board shorts parade,
A seagull steals chips; I'm afraid!
Someone's boat drifted, what a mess,
It's the fish that could care less.

The moonbeam's shine lights up my drink,
I mix it up, with lemon blink.
Around me laughter takes a flight,
A night of fun, oh what a sight!

Sandwich fights and silly cheers,
The jelly truly hits my gears.
As waves brush close, I shout, "Oh dear!"
This beach is wild, let's kick it here!

## Whispered Dreams in the Sea Breeze

The ocean murmurs tales so sly,
A sea lion winks – is he shy?
I slip and slide across the shore,
The tide's embrace, forevermore.

With conch shells tuning in to tease,
I find some driftwood, oh what a breeze!
Each grain of sand has got a face,
As I stumble, I misplace my grace.

Seashells giggle at my plight,
While fireworks pop, oh what a sight!
Mermaids laugh behind our backs,
Plotting schemes and silly hacks.

Underneath the starry cloak,
I toast with juice, spill, oh choke!
Giggles echo from afar,
Let's dance with dreams, wherever they are!

## Crystal Waves and Shimmering Light

Waves crash in with playful might,
I lose my hat in a gusty flight.
Surfboards wobble, people glide,
I steer wrong, must be my pride.

Sparkles dance upon the sea,
As I get splashed, oh joy, whee!
Crustaceans giggle, making fun,
This beach is wild, let's all run!

A dolphin bubbles, "Join the dance!"
While sandcastle's under chance.
I've built a tower, or so I thought,
But the tide says, "Nope! I've got!"

So here we are, in this fine place,
With sunny smiles on every face.
Let laughter roll like waves of cheer,
In this wild sea, let's disappear!

## The Ocean's Breath at Dawn

The waves roll in, they tickle my toes,
A jellyfish wiggles, where no one goes.
Seagulls squawk loudly, with their breakfast schemes,
While I sip my coffee, pondering dreams.

The rising sun paints the sky in gold,
I find a lost flip-flop, worth a fortune untold.
A crab scuttles by, like he owns the sand,
And I laugh out loud at his princely stand.

The ocean breathes deeply, in melodious sighs,
While seaweed does the cha-cha, under brightening skies.

A fish jumps high, with no grace or style,
As I shake my head, trying hard not to smile.

So here I sit, with my toes in the sea,
The tide's my best buddy, forever carefree.
With each silly wave, life's troubles take flight,
As the ocean and I share this hilarious sight.

## A Dance of Driftwood

Driftwood twirls, in a ballet of waves,
Winking at kids, who think it's so brave.
A starfish snaps selfies, tweeting with flair,
While barnacles gossip, they just don't care.

The tide lifts its arms, for a twist and a turn,
A seagull takes center, it's his time to yearn.
Swirling in laughter, the tide does a spin,
As splashes of water spray all over my chin.

With a clam for a partner, the dance floor's alive,
They two-step so clumsily, it's hard to survive.
A turtle joins in, with his slow little groove,
And I'm on the shore, in my own silly move.

So join in the fun, it's a wacky frolic,
With driftwood and seashells, it's nothing but frolic.
Under the sun, let your laughter flow free,
For life's just a dance, on this beach jubilee.

## Solitude Beneath the Stars

Under the stars, the ocean winks bright,
A crab sings a tune, in the cool of the night.
The moon is a lantern, it glows on the sea,
As a dolphin plays peek-a-boo, just for me.

I sit on the sand, feeling salt on my skin,
A beach ball rolls by, with a chuckle and grin.
The stars whisper secrets, tales of the tide,
While I try to catch fish, though they run and hide.

The shore's full of puzzles, like seashells and stones,
And a rogue wave steals my snacks, oh, how it moans!
My sandwich goes floating, a very brief trip,
As laughter erupts from my surprised lips.

So here's to the night, with a silly old flair,
With crabs holding karaoke, and seaweed frizzed hair.
Alone but not lonely, with giggles a-plenty,
In the moonlit embrace, life feels all too zesty.

## **Where Sea Meets Sky**

Where the blue kisses blue, both swim and unite,
A mermaid juggles pearls, what a strange sight!
Clouds float like boats, sails ready to go,
While the sun plays peek-a-boo, putting on quite the show.

Waves raise their voices, a raucous delight,
As fish flip and flop, with pure fishy might.
The horizon tickles, as seagulls all shout,
A flock of them hustling, what's that all about?

I spy a lost sandal, the tide's favorite game,
As whispers of sandcastles call out my name.
Each grain has a story, of beaches bygone,
Unraveling laughter, with each silly dawn.

So here we frolic, where water meets air,
The ocean's a carnival, with wonders to share.
With a splash of humor, and a glimmering eye,
Life's an adventure, where we all laugh and try.

## The lullaby of Little Shells

Little shells dance on the sand,
They hold secrets from the deep, grand.
With a wink and a tiny swirl,
They giggle like a bashful girl.

Each one makes a chirpy sound,
Simply laughing, feeling proud.
A shell parade is on display,
With crabs in tuxedos joining the fray.

Seagulls swoop in with flair,
Wearing hats, what a sight, I swear!
They tap dance on the wooden pier,
And ask the shells, "Can we join here?"

As the tide giggles like a child,
Nature's jesters are running wild.
In the sun's warm embrace, they play,
A silly show for a blissful day.

## Caress of the Salted Breeze

The salted breeze whispers a joke,
As it tickles your nose, awoke.
It sways the kites that soar on high,
While they laugh and spin in the sky.

The sandcastles melt like ice cream,
With a saltwater splash, a silly dream.
Waves crash in with a playful roar,
Chasing flip-flops to the ocean's floor.

Seashells gossip about the tide,
Their tiny stories, a laughing guide.
The wind replies with a playful spin,
Inviting you to dance and grin.

So let the breeze ruffle your hair,
And let your worries drift in the air.
At the beach, life's a chuckle-filled rise,
With every wave, hear the laughter flies.

## Echoes of a Quiet Coast

On a quiet coast, a crab takes a stroll,
Waving claws like a dapper patrol.
Shells are cheering from the ground,
As the crab wobbles round and round.

A hermit crab sneaks in a shell,
Claiming, "This fits me quite well!"
But the shell laughs and rolls away,
"Sorry, buddy, I'm done for the day!"

The sun giggles, painting the sea,
With warm colors that shout, "Look at me!"
A sandpiper hops, oh what a sight,
With tiny feet that dance with delight.

Echoes of laughter fill the air,
As seagulls join in without a care.
At the coast, humor's laid-back and free,
A joyful symphony, just let it be.

## Morning Light on the Water

Morning light tickles the waves,
As fishy friends play in tiny caves.
They splash about like kids at noon,
Chasing rays, singing to the moon.

A dolphin prances, a comedic show,
Juggling seaweed, oh what a pro!
He flips and flops in a quirky line,
Sending bubbles that sparkle and shine.

The sun peeks over, a golden grin,
Warming up the world, let the fun begin!
With each ripple, a giggle flows,
As playful surf whispers tales, it knows.

So grab your hat and join the fun,
As the day wakes up, under the sun.
With laughter in waves and smiles aglow,
Morning's promise, come join the show!

## Sailboats Gliding into the Horizon

Sailboats glide, like cats on snooze,
Drifting past the laughing cruise.
Their captains wave, with drink in hand,
As seagulls cheer, that perfect band.

Sunshine winks, the waves a tease,
While turtles dance, with utmost ease.
Fish swim by, they laugh and gloat,
At the sight of a flapping coat.

Crabs wear shades, on sandy throne,
While mermaids giggle, in a tone.
A lighthouse beams, a wink of light,
To boats that giggle at the sight.

The ocean's pulse, a rhythmic tune,
As rubber ducks, float under moon.
A jellyfish, with disco moves,
Hosts a party, with splendid grooves.

## An Invitation to Listen to the Waves

Hey there, friend, lend me your ear,
The waves have gossip, oh so dear.
They whisper tales of salty blunders,
That make you laugh and gasp with wonders.

"Once, a dolphin wore a hat!
He lost it dancing, what of that?"
A starfish chimes, "It's quite unfair,
I'm stuck here with sand in my hair!"

The crabs hold court, with shells for crowns,
Sharing secrets of seaweed towns.
They crack jokes, and all of us sway,
At the tidal wave's playful display.

So let's gather 'round, don't be shy,
For the ocean's giggles are passing by.
With laughter echoing through each spray,
The waves will share their humor today.

## Smiles of Sand Dollars

In the sun, sand dollars shine bright,
With happy faces, what a sight!
They wish to tell their sandy tales,
Of mermaid parties and dolphin trails.

One said, "I had a hat once too,
But a seagull thought it was for stew!"
Another chimed, "I'm all about peace,
Just don't step on me, I'll call for cease!"

Together they laugh, in grains of gold,
Sharing secrets never told.
With winks and smiles they roll with glee,
Sand dollars' joy, how great to be free!

Take a moment, bend down low,
Catch a glimpse of their cheeky glow.
They're treasures found, with humor rife,
Sand dollars smiling, oh what a life!

## Nature's Poetry in the Breaking Waves

Listen close, the waves compose,
Silly sonnets that nobody knows.
A frothy laugh, a bubbly cheer,
Nature's poets, loud and clear.

With every splash, a word takes flight,
As shells join in, what pure delight!
A clam sings bass, as terns hum tunes,
And barnacles dance, beneath the moons.

"Roses are red, violets are blue,
We're all poetical, how about you?"
Said a surfing seal with a wink so sly,
"Join our class, don't just pass by!"

Every tide brings verses anew,
In hiccupping waves, and glistening dew.
So come along, and ride the flow,
For nature's box of jokes will glow!

# Footprints in Eternal Sand

I left my marks where waves ran free,
A crab marched by, said, "Hey, look at me!"
My footprints danced in silly formation,
While seagulls laughed at my grand migration.

As the tide crept up, my prints disappeared,
"Too late!" I cried, the ocean sneered.
With every splash, I thought it quite grand,
I put my foot down and lost my last stand.

The lesson learned on this sunny spree,
Waves are quite bold, they've no sense of glee.
I waved goodbye to my sandy brigade,
While fish nearby chuckled and then played.

So if you wander near seaside delight,
Know tides will snicker with all of their might.
Next time I'll tread with shoes that can float,
And leave behind a funnier note!

## Serene Tide Pools at Dawn

At dawn I peered in pools so deep,
Found starfish posing, oh what a heap!
A hermit crab waved from a damp little door,
"My shell's bigger than yours!" He opened the floor.

An octopus slick with a sheen of surprise,
Took my coffee donut, a brave little prize.
As I laughed at the scene, slipped on a wet rock,
The tide pool grinned, I was nature's big joke!

With bubbles a-bouncing and laughter anew,
Seaweed danced wildly, it joined in, too.
Those creatures gasped as I slipped and twirled,
Creating a splash, oh, my antics unfurled!

So next time you visit those calm, silly pools,
Wear funny boots, like oversized tools.
For nature may giggle at all your charades,
And grant you adventures that laughter parades!

## The Quiet Song of Pebbled Shores

On pebbled shores where my slippers squeak,
I hummed a tune that was far from chic.
The stones all whispered, "We need better songs!"
But I tripped on a pebble and proved them all wrong!

The crabs tapped along with their sideways stride,
A conch shell laughed; I could hardly abide.
The waves joined in with a rhythmic embrace,
While clams clapped their shells like they won the big race!

With flat rocks as my stage, I danced like a fool,
Those pebbles and creatures thought me the jewel.
"Encore!" yelled the tide as I slipped on my pattern,
The laughter of shells made me feel like a hatter.

So when next you stroll on the stony domain,
Don't be shy, let your awkwardness reign.
For laughter is a song all its own, my dear,
And the quiet of shores sings loudly, I fear!

## Windswept Dreams Along the Coast

On breezy days, my hat took flight,
Soaring through clouds, what a silly sight!
I chased after dreams, my arms flailed wide,
The seagulls just cawed, not a pinch of pride.

The wind played tricks, a true jokester's game,
Brought sand to my face, oh what a shame!
Caught in a gust, my shorts flew askew,
Locked in a battle, the wind boldly blew.

My laugh echoed out, a comical cheer,
While beachgoers gasped as I stumbled near.
They joined in the fun, tossed their worries aside,
In the windy embrace, we all took a ride!

So if you wander where breezes abound,
Be ready for laughter and treasures unbound.
For in every gust, there's a giggle in tow,
And dreams that are windswept can truly bestow!

## Essence of Gentle Waves Flowing

The waves tickle toes, oh what a tease,
Seagulls squawk gossip, brought by the breeze.
With sand in my shoes, I dance in delight,
A crab scuttles past, giving me a fright!

The sun wears sunglasses, all cool and bright,
Shells whisper secrets, they're out for a bite.
I chase after kites that fly overhead,
Then trip on my towel, landing face-first in bread!

With each splash and laugh, the moments we keep,
The tide tells a joke, in waves soft and deep.
Life's better when sandy, feeling so spry,
I'll savor this fun, as gulls laugh on high!

So here on the coast, where the wild things roam,
I find all my joy, I feel right at home.
With each gentle wave, my worries I stave,
Happiness flows, like the sea — I behave!

## Horizons Unfurled in Solitude

On this vast expanse, I spot a lone shoe,
Looks like someone's left it; oh, what's it been through?
The sun's on vacation, it's taking a dip,
I join in the fun, let my troubles just skip.

A fish eyeing me, with curiosity bright,
I wiggle and wave, causing quite the sight.
The clouds play peek-a-boo, hiding my sun,
Each crease of the horizon, a laughter-filled run!

With a breeze in my hair and sand on my nose,
I spot a lost flip-flop; where did it go?
Whispers of waves, they jest and they sway,
While the horizon giggles, just keeping at bay.

In solitude's embrace, jokes come to unfold,
Each chuckle with waves; a treasure of gold.
So let's dance with the tide, let's swim with the flow,
For here by the sea, we find joy in the woe!

## The Beauty of Still Waters Running

A duck in a sunhat floats by with great flair,
It quacks to the rhythm, what style! What rare!
Reflections dance quietly, laughing at me,
While I try to look serious — oh, can't you see?

The ripples do giggle, splashing nearby,
They chuckle and snicker as I trip and fly.
With a stick as my scepter, I reign over pond,
While frogs in tuxedos nod with a bond.

The lilies wear crowns, gossip sweetly in bloom,
As I wade through the water, creating a zoom.
Searching for fish, but they outsmart my gaze,
They swim like they're dancers, performing their plays!

Still waters, they shimmer with jokes to unmask,
Each secret, each ripple, is all I could ask.
With laughter abound and joy never done,
In beauty's embrace, oh, we all have such fun!

## Lighthouses Guarding Dreams

The lighthouse stands tall, with a hat of bright white,
It guards against pirates that dance in the night.
A beam full of laughter, it sweeps 'cross the bay,
While seagulls play tag and the fish swim away!

With each turn of the light, it signals the way,
"Hurry up now, folks, there's a joke to relay!"
The boats wave back, with a wink and a cheer,
As the humor sails in, far and near.

Under the stars, the lighthouse starts to hum,
It cracks silly puns about how waves can drum.
A guardian of giggles, a beacon of glee,
In the heart of the sea, it sets our minds free!

So let's gather our dreams on this magical coasts,
With lighthouses guiding and laughter, our hosts.
For each wave that crashes, a joy that redeems,
In this dance of the tide, we treasure our dreams!

## Harmonies in the Rolling Surf

The tide rolls in, then goes back out,
Seagulls sing of fish, with wings, they shout.
A crab does a dance, oh what a scene,
While beach lovers stumble just like they've seen!

Sand castles crumble, they're not quite grand,
A flip flop flies, oh isn't that planned?
Kids laugh and chase as the waves do tease,
Ice cream drips down with the greatest of ease!

A dog digs deep in the shifting sand,
Paws flying everywhere, quite unplanned.
Who knew that laughter could ride the breeze?
Such comedy found by the swaying trees!

As day fades out and stars come to play,
The ocean's giggles carry far away.
In waves of chuckles, the night draws near,
And moonlit moments bring joy and cheer.

## Seaglass Memories and Quiet Thoughts

Fragments of green shine on sandy floor,
Memories linger, like tales from yore.
A bottle rolls by, a message inside,
But all that we find are just jokes to abide!

Old flip flops whisper, "How's your day been?"
"Not too bad," says one, "I just lost a friend!"
Buried treasures, you stumble and trip,
"Hey watch it!" they yell, while you just flip!

Waves tumble in, with laughter they beckon,
A seagull steals fries, the sneaky little Wreckin'!
Quiet thoughts drift like clouds in the sky,
While beach chairs tip over, oh my my!

As the sun dips low, we gather on the shore,
Reliving the giggles, who could ask for more?
With toes in the sand and hearts full of glee,
This strange beach life feels just like a spree!

## Calm Currents of the Soul

The ocean whispers secrets in forms of waves,
While jellyfish float like translucent knaves.
With starfish applauding, they cheer and sway,
As sunbathers sneeze, tossing sand in dismay.

Dolphins leap high, tipping hat to the sun,
"Sunburns and laughter, we're just here for fun!"
Floating on rafts, we sip lemonade flows,
And sunscreen's the title to battle our woes!

Seashells tell stories of daydreams and flights,
Of sandbar parties lasting through the nights.
A crab flips a burger – do they not see?
The grill's not for crabs, old buddy, just be!

Let currents of chuckles fill hearts and minds,
As laughter floats freely with soft evening winds.
With one last giggle, we bid the day's end,
And dance with the twilight, our friend 'til amend!

## **Glistening Horizons at Daybreak**


The sun peeks up and yawns at the sea,
Waves tickle the shore, it's so carefree!
A seagull squawks loudly, "Who's up for a run?"
While barnacles grumble, "We just want some fun!"

As coffee's brewed, the mugs do collide,
"Let's make it a contest," one says with pride!
Saltwater spills from a cheeky water spout,
And beachballs pop louder than a seagull shout!

Shells scatter joy like confetti in air,
Like nature's confessions held under a flair.
As surfboards parade in their morning glory,
The sun rises up, it's just one big story!

With laughter as bright as the dawn's early light,
The endless horizon calls out with delight.
So let's chase those giggles wherever they lead,
In this wacky world, we will all take heed!

## Where the Sands Meet the Sky

The seagulls squawk, a fishy chat,
Waves dance and play while I sit flat.
A crab in my flip-flop makes a break,
I laugh so hard, my sandwich shakes.

The sunbeams tease my sunburnt nose,
A pail of jokes beside me flows.
The sand's too hot for my toes to bare,
I juggle ice cream, it's a slippery affair.

Just a beach bum in a straw hat,
With a jellyfish that thinks I'm a mat.
As I run from the tide, I trip and splash,
An awkward ballet—oh, what a crash!

Now I lie here, a sandcastle king,
Beneath a sky that starts to sing.
I wave to the clouds, they wave right back,
Together we giggle, that's our knack!

## Moonlit Murmurs of the Bay

The moon winks down, a glowing light,
As crabs do the tango, what a sight!
Starfish gossip, they're quite the crew,
I join in, too, with my flip-flop shoe.

The surf sings low, a whispering tune,
While seaweed dances under the moon.
I try to join, but trip on a tail,
Splashing my dreams, they float like a sail.

With laughter echoing through the night,
I spot a dolphin—oh, what a fright!
It jumps and spins, full of flair,
I bow in awe, now how did it dare?

The waves applaud with a bubbly cheer,
As I moonwalk awkwardly near.
The bay's alive with whispers of fun,
Under the moon, we gleefully run!

## **Stillness Beneath the Salt Spray**

Where quiet moments find their space,
A dog in a hat runs with grace.
Salt on my lips, a smile so wide,
As a bird steals chips, oh, I can't hide!

The breezy air brushes my cheeks,
As I sit back and enjoy the peaks.
A wave shouts softly, 'Catch me if you can!'
I attempt a splash; instead, I'm a pan.

Surfers ride high, they're brave and bold,
While I tease the tide with tales retold.
A jellyfish drifts by, oh-so-sly,
I swear it winked, just like a guy!

Stillness reigns but laughter's spread,
With crabs as my audience, all have said.
Here in the retreat of salty spray,
Life's a grand joke—let's all play!

## Dance of Shadows on the Beach

Beneath the sun, the shadows play,
As I trip over nothing—a graceful sway.
The dunes decide to host a show,
Where I'm the star, but crushed by a toe!

Sandcastles tower, grandiose dreams,
But the tide sneaks in, oh, how it gleams!
With a splash and a rush, it wipes them out,
I stand in awe, and then start to pout.

The shadows of palm trees stretch and yawn,
While I'm busy attempting to brawn.
A frisbee flies by, grazing my head,
Oops, looks like dancing's out of my thread!

But I laugh with the waves, twirling around,
For every mishap's a joy to be found.
With friends by my side in this peaceful scene,
We dance in the sand, like we're all mean!

## **Leaves Dancing to the Ocean's Rhapsody**

Leaves spin like tops, in a dizzy delight,
Seagulls wear shades, it's a comical sight.
They twirl with the wind, in a chortling spree,
Nature's own dance, in the salty sea breeze.

Crabs hold a limbo, while fish try to groove,
The tide plays the music, they just have to move.
With shells as their stage, they strut and they prance,
Even the barnacles join in the dance!

A jellyfish wobbles, a true heavyweight,
While seaweed takes selfies, feeling so great.
Turtles are chuckling at the things they see,
In this watery world of pure jubilee.

So next time you wander, along ocean's way,
Watch for the laughter, it might just convey.
That nature's a jester, in sun and in foam,
Inviting us all to feel right at home.

## The Warmth of Sun-Kissed Sands

Sun-kissed sands giggle, as toes touch their face,
They tickle your feet, in a bright, cheeky race.
"Step right up, buddy," they seem to implore,
"Dive in our warmth! Who could ask for more?"

Beach towels unfold like a blanket of cheer,
With sunscreen in hand, 'it's time for a smear!'
The seagulls are swooping, like they own the place,
Stealing hot fries with an expert-like grace.

Sandcastles sprout wings, ready for flight,
With moats made of giggles, oh what a sight!
A bucket and spade form a mightily team,
Taking on waves in a childish dream.

So lay back and laugh on this canvas of gold,
Where stories are spun, oh so silly and bold.
Feel the sun's warm embrace, let your worries unwind,
In the joy of these sands, pure laughter you'll find.

## Harmony in the Creak of Driftwood

Driftwood's been strumming, a tune all its own,
As waves gently clapped, it felt like a throne.
A guitar made of bark, with barnacles too,
Nature's own band, with a wild, salty crew!

Each creak sets the rhythm, a natural beat,
With starfish as fans, they're groovin' in heat.
A crab plays the maracas, shaking with flair,
While a clam drops the bass with a rhythmic care.

The dolphins are dancing, sending splashes on cue,
As sea breeze fills sails, with a laughter so true.
In this concert of life, all creatures partake,
Making memories countless, that never will break.

So lean on that driftwood, let laughter unfold,
Join this grand jam where stories are told.
In harmony, found where the sea meets the land,
With nature's wild orchestra, isn't it grand?

## Nurturing the Silence of the Sea

The waves whisper secrets, in a voice low and sweet,
Bubbles burst laughing, at the game of hide and seek.
Crabs hold their breath, as shadows drift by,
In this game of the quiet, who will fly high?

Seashells play poker, with sand as the pot,
Counting their treasures, oh what have they got?
In this calm little world, where giggles abound,
The silence of the sea, is humor profound.

Turtles in slow-mo, just taking their time,
While fish crack a joke, in a splashy rhyme.
Urchins roll laughter, as they tumble around,
In the nurturing silence, joy is profound.

So pause at this moment, let stillness set free,
Listen close, my friend, to the humor of the sea.
For in every soft tide, and wave's gentle sway,
Lies a world of laughter, waiting to play.

www.ingramcontent.com/pod-product-compliance
Lightning Source LLC
Chambersburg PA
CBHW072129070526
44585CB00016B/1597